CW00833076

EVAGATORY

EVAGATORY

Peter Reading

Chatto & Windus
LONDON

Published in 1992 by
Chatto & Windus Ltd.
20 Vauxhall Bridge Road
London SW1V 2SA

A CIP catalogue record for this book is available
from the British Library

ISBN 0 7011 3924 2

For/facilitated by the Lannan Foundation

Photoset by
Cambridge Composing (UK) Ltd
Cambridge

Printed in Great Britain by
Mackays of Chatham PLC,
Chatham, Kent

Doyle's on the harbour, dusk, pulse of warning light,
octopus, crayfish, chill gold dry semillon's
    bouquet of ripe grapes/pollen; plum-mauve
      Rothko of afterglow on which silent
slow-flapping fruit-bats' transient silhouettes. . .

      a.m., a carcinogenic sunrise
    (**15% of population. . .**),
shrieking, an iridescence of lorikeets
raucous from palms and blossoming eucalypts;
Sydney, *The Age* screwed up in a trash-bucket.

8 a.m., Hobart, bar of the Ship Hotel.
Over their ice-cold Cascades a couple of
        shicks are discussing Nubeena, Wedge Bay,
    Oakwood, Port Arthur, Highcroft, Stormlea,
    how, in the Convict Ruins, wylahs
(yellow-tailed black, funereal cockatoos,
    Calyptorhynchus funereus),
    wailing their weird *wee-yu wy-la*, are
    really the ghosts of sun-charred hanged cons.

Tew that kindley Chaplaing
whot preechis in Port After:
Sir, I gets hangd this day,
me as wus transportud
back in '37
(then ajed onley 16)
tew New Serf Wails, escaped,
become bushranjer, catched,
sent Port After, neerly
scaped agin – this time
sent Nofuck Isle, rebelld,
sentenst tew be hangd.
But I was wonce humayne,
drove tew desparayshun
by crewelty of prizzin.
Strong ties of erth wil soon
be renched, this burnin fever
of life wil soon be kwenched,
mi grayve wil be a haven,
a restern plays fer me,
Wil Westwood, sir, from cup
of mizry hav I drank
from 16th yeer, ten long
yeeers, the sweetest drarft
is that as takes away
mizry of livin deth.
I welcum deth – a frend
as do deceyve no man –
and all shall then be qiyet,
no tyrant wil disturb
repoze, I hope. I now
do bid the world A Due
and all as it contaynes!

Pipe Clay Lagoon, wet silver ellipse of sand
pulsing in lightwaves, pure cerulean dome,
     indigo-bruised smooth straits of turquoise,
bloodshot-eyed *Larus novaehollandiae*,

delicacies laid out on a linen cloth,
     crusty bread, avocados, smoked quails,
          crisp knots of lettuce, terrine of salmon,
     raspberries, pinot noir Moorilla,

resinous pine shade under an ozone hole
     (one of those routine periodic
faunal extinctions [cf. the Cambrian]),
     eucalypts shred-barked, parched buff hectares.

26 hours of 747-lag,
touchdown to Greenhouse meteorology,
          wind preternatural, pissing acid.

Down from the sleet-clad mountains into
        Mostar, fecundity (pulsing UV
irradiating vines, figs, peaches).

Carp baked in herbs and bijelo vino,
carcass of whole lamb spiked on a slow-turned spit
over sweet pine-smoke outside a crumbling bar.

Long after midnight, crno vino,
visokokvalitetno vino,
        vinjak, strings strummed by a frost-haired elder,
Jasmina mouthing soft-breathed translationese:

This is his song's weight, Time's malice castigates
        not only me (whose beard grows snow-hued,
        bones become joint-sore, dulled eyes gum-filled),
                also fair governments, concepts, zeniths,
        all which we valued nears expiry.

Midnight, an open window in Trebinje,
    thrashing of warm May rain on fig leaves,
nightingale, one hour richly mellifluous
    under this vitriolated downpour.

Café Dalmacija, Adriatic
violet (dark as crno vino),
liquorice-bitter gritty coffee,
vinjac, Jasmina's whispered translation of
lyrical twang from a grizzled oldie:

Surely Odysseus roamed these blithe isles,
parsley and iris cushioning meadowlands,
fumous the scents of split cypress, juniper,
vine-stems rich-clustered, temptress voluptuous,
touched by salacious caresses [silence,
scanning with tears a barren expanse of sea],
knowing delights venereal, lachrymose.

ye haue heard this yarn afore
(but I'm minded on it againe
thefe daies of fqualls and rank clouds
and raines as is vitriolic –
pines fhorn ftark as mizzen-mafts
wi neuer a frolicfome fowl –
and ye top-gallant air all rent):

how we was one Monday anchored
off Mafcarenhas Iflande
in fourteen fathom o water;
how, feeking diuerfion, we landed;
how, on ye trees, there was pigeons
as blue as polifhed flate
which fuffered vs, being fo tame,
for to pluck em iuft like fruits
from ye branches and pull their necks;
how we killed two hundred firft day;
how we alfo killed grey paraquets
(moft entertayninge to cetch
a grey paraquet and *twift* it
fo as it fqueals aloud
till ye reft of its kind flock round,
therevpon themfelues being cetched);
how there was alfo penguins
(which laft hath but ftumps for wings,
fo being ye eafier to kill)
which we killed above four hundred;
how there was alfo wild geefe
and turtles above an hundred;
how we killed all thefe and more;
and ye Tuefday more and more;
and ye Wednefday more and more;
and ye Thurfday more and more;
ye haue heard this yarn afore

Came to an island farctate with feculence:
chip-papers, Diet-Pepsi cans clattering,
prams, supermarket trolleys, spent mattresses,

bus-rank of steel and rank uriniferous
concrete, a footbridge richly enlivened with
    aerosol squirtings, daubed graffiti,

        pustular simian sub-teenagers
    hurling abuse and empty bottles
        over the parapet into crowds of
        pensioners waiting for **X-PRESS SERVISS,**

        xylophone tinkle of smashed glass, crackle
    under a tyre, a hapless old fart
    stanching the flow from freshly sliced flesh.

Avian botulism thriving
(black plastic bin-bags/scavenging *Laridae*);
   sand-eels depleted (over-fishing):

sanitized quondam herring gull colony,
sanitized quondam kittiwake colony –
   all that remains, their last year's shit's stink.

53 bus approaching the terminus;
    dapper sartorial English elder
   suited in Manx tweed, close-clipped grey tash:

Too much is wrong, Gibbonian undertones,
    schooling and bread and dress and manners,
era's decline, Elgarian sadnesses;

too much is wrong, duff ticker, insomnia,
    ulcer and thyrotoxicosis,
        end of the world in one's lifetime likely,
flight of a sparrow brief through the feasting hall.

Perilous trek, unarmed, unaccompanied:
    set out from Cranium, through uncharted
  swamp, to arrive at Lingua Franca,
thence to this Logaoedic Dependency.

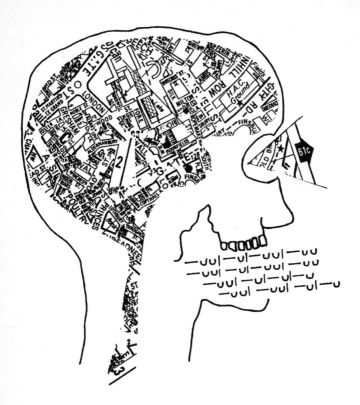

Cranial voice loquacious/inadequate
    (translationese from life to lingo):

Only a troubled idyll now possible,
pastoral picnic under an ozone hole,
England, *The Times* screwed up in a trash-bucket,
    gliding astern, the Thames, the old prides,
    end of an era, nation, notion,
        Albion urban, devenustated
    (one of those routine periodic
faunal extinctions [cf. the Permian]),
arthropod aberration (posterity).

a dreadful, bloody, civil insurrection among the poor mad islanders brought about because their automobiles, which they had revered above all else, and which had helped boost their weak, inferior egos, had been confiscated by their (suddenly aware and panic-stricken) government. For it seems that, whereas the manifest absurdity of mayhem on congested tarmac and the lowering mantle of ferruginous fog had somehow failed to awaken authoritarian sensibility, this abrupt (albeit long-prognosticated) termination of a fundamental, unrenewable

Newspapers there (the sumps of society,
draining off, holding up for inspection a
   corporate concentrated slurry)
retail, with relish, mayhem and muck of a
      clapped-out, subliterate, scrap-stuffed fake state:
   23.3 million vehicles,
   29.8 million drivers,
300 000 maimed on their ludicrous
   tarmac p.a., 5000 flenched dead –
      fortunate, then, that it doesn't matter
(for they are far too philoprogenitive).

Snow-haired, an elder, dulled eyes gum-filled,
tuning a sweet-toned curious instrument,
     gulps from a goblet of local merlot,
     sings on a theme whose fame was fabled,
that of a sad realm farctate with feculence
     (patois and translationese alternately):

Gobschighte damapetty,
   gobby Fer-dama,
   getspeeke baggsy,
   getspeeke parly
   comma cul, comma
   malbicker-bicker,
porky getspeeke?, porky?

Wonderful little Madam,
self-mocking Iron Lady,
who some said was a windbag,
some said talked
like an arsehole, like
a termagant – why,
why did some say that?

Pascoz vots clobberjoli,
   vots chevvy-dur dur,
   vots baggsymain chic,
   vots collier-prick,
   cuntyvach twitnit,
   iscst pukkerjoli –
illos jalouz dats porky!

Because your pretty frocks,
your permed-stiff hair,
your smart handbag, your
tight-sharp necklace,
satrapess so marvellous,
were so beautiful –
they were envious, that's it!

Ni iscst vots marrypappa
   grignaleto, ne.
   Mas vots pollytiq
   saggio sauvay
   vots salinsula,
   insulapetty,
et fair tutts egal mit-nochts.

Nor was your spouse
a pipsqueak – far from it!
But your many wise policies
were saving your islet,
your filthy isle, and
made all equal with nil.

East End of London, where the indigenous
        practise a noteworthy brand of homicide –
fruit and veg hurled from speeding limos.
Melons, potatoes, cauliflowers, aubergines,
clutter the vegetarian headlines here:
        Turnip tops septuagenarian shopper,
    Juvenile jogger culled by cabbage.

Forest, Sarawak, limestone outcrop,
caverns of roosting Bornean horseshoe bats
(faeces of which are sifted by cockroaches);

one-and-a-half miles into the labyrinth,
    reservoir, stalactitic vaulting,
etiolated, eyeless crustacean,
        wheeze of a Tilley lamp near expiry.

    Guideless, directionless, lightless, silence.

Edge of black Baltic, night, north-easter,
        low-ceilinged candle-lit gloomy *keller*,
flocculent-headed yeast-fragrant beer, a bench,
        basins of pork-dripping, coarse sour rye-bread,
        Germanic drone of a drunk salt's slurred dirge,
whisper of scented soft-breathed translationese:

Mine is a sea-borne sorrowful history,
        winters of toil through tempests, foam frosts,
        fearing the future's vicious voyage,
        lashing of iced brine, hurled hail, waves' thrash,
longing for land and cuckoo's sad call of spring. . .

                nothing on earth can abide forever,
                illness or age or aggression takes us,
                striving for fame beyond death is futile
(none will be left to celebrate heroes' *lof*),

days and delights depart, and inferior
        beings infest and despoil earth, each one
        greys and grows grave and, pallid, passes.

. . .dawn of each day I bewail my sorrows,
    how I was sundered in youth from homelands

[fuelled by a yeast-frothed litre, a wandering
    dosser drones on in 'the local lingo],

no man grows wise without many winters spent
    pondering folly of worthless world's-gear,

awful the apprehension of earth-ending,
    crumbled the mead-hall, no laugh lasting,

where are the heroes, word-hoarders, feasting-feats? —
gone back to dark as though they had never been,

life is a loan and bank accounts transient,
    kindred are skewered on sharp-spiked ash-spears,

    all of this world will be Weird-wreaked,
                    emptied. . .

Province of hyperborean bleakness,
    Cranium. Roused by nightmare (in which
I am a butcher, cleaver repeatedly
    hacking your carcass, five-years-dead friend),
grief gushes raw again from an old lesion.

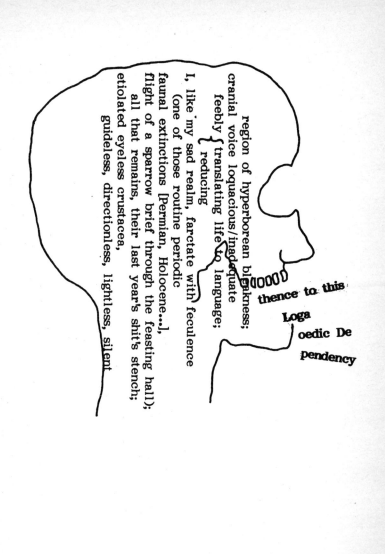

region of hyperborean bleakness;
cranial voice loquacious/inadequate
feebly { translating life to language;
       { reducing
I, like my sad realm, farctate with feculence
  (one of those routine periodic
faunal extinctions [Permian, Holocene...],
flight of a sparrow brief through the feasting hall);
all that remains, their last year's shit's stench;
etiolated eyeless crustacea,
  guideless, directionless, lightless, silent

thence to this
Loga
oedic De
pendency

upon an island where the natives venerated a deity. It was soon apprehended that the object of their adoration was a species of duck, *Anas platyrhynchos* (the mallard). Anyone unenlightened enough to revere, say, the pochard (*Aythya ferina*), the wigeon (*Anas penelope*) or the smew (*Mergus albellus*) was subjected to corrective interrogation by a most venerable committee and, invariably, sentenced to suffer personal destruction.

There was one in that place, cowering in the police-protected exile of a concrete bunker, who had advocated, ill-advisedly, the omniscient immutability of the velvet scoter (*Melanitta fusca*), and

Prouerbes xiij. iij

He that infults Our Mallard muft pay for it;
hee that reueres falfe pochard and blafphemous
wigeon and fmew knows not Yᵉ True Quack
which was reuealed to vs by Our Drake's
beak.

Therefore a Iiffy bag plump with correctiue plaftic
explofiue
plops on yᵉ mat with yᵉ mail, blafts his child's face
into pulp.

[Hee who keeps fhtum ftays aliue.]

Waded ashore, St. Pancras Isle, 2 a.m.,
    knee-deep in poly burger-boxes,
    black plastic bin-bags, spat snot, spilt pils.

    Cushioned in mulch from trash-skips' spillage
    (cabbage fronds, glass shards, date-expired cakes),
        calmly a couple coited, stirred by
    conviviality [or copecks].

Came to an island whereon the natives make
caps (worn by prankster drolls) on the peaks of which,
   gleaming, repose the simulacra,
      sculpted in plastic, of great big dog turds.
   Thus are they designated: **Shitheads**.

Sham-rustic lair of quondam Parnassian
(lapsed into silence – like great Sibelius,
mute till the end – reflective of wordlessness);

vinous-rich wallflowers, arbour, a wicker chair
        in the last corner receiving sunlight;
      evening, a violet-shadowed sad shire
      running to exponential ruin
(not enough condoms, too many mountain bikes);

voice in the head loquacious/inadequate
      glibly enumerating mayhem
      (prettily pyrotechnic oilfields,
Cape Grim recording ozone-depleting air,
progeny guaranteed a climacteric);

only a troubled idyll now possible,
      few of the better years remaining. . .
'55 Margaux, '61 Léoville.

Blizzard, Niagara, roaring white-out,
cast iron scrolls of parapet frozen like
   ammonite whorls in waxed ice matrix.

Mountainous Franco-Italian border,
Tende, medieval, steep labyrinthine wynds,
bell-tower surmounting rough terracotta-roofed
   hovels, a terraced graveyard, tombs like
      hundreds of matrices pierced with snap-shots.

Our craft approaching yᵉfhore,
many fcores of diuers fowls,
all clagged in fome fticky tar,
did flacker away from yᵉ land;
foon we was able to fee
yᵉ aquatic graffes all fered,
likewife all nature of flora;
fifhes vp-bellied and white
in a noifome vifcous fwell,
for, in truth, yᵉ waues was black,
yᵉ furface a floating fcum;
on running athwart a ridge
of rock, when we feared our fkiff
muft fpring a breach in her caulk,
rather, yᵉ fable stone
did crumble like iet meringue;
now preternatural fqualls
did moderate, and ftrange vapours
defcend in ferruginous fog,
an oppreffiue heat, withal;
then did we verily know
we had entered vnto Yᵉ Gulph.

     region of hyperborean bleakness;
cranial voice loquacious/inadequate
    feebly   { translating life to language;
             reducing
I, like my sad realm, farctate with feculence
    (one of those routine periodic
faunal extinctions [Permian, Holocene. . .],
flight of a sparrow brief through the feasting hall,
    all that remains, their last year's shit's stench),
etiolated eyeless crustacean,
    etiolated aberration,
        guideless, directionless, lightless, silent

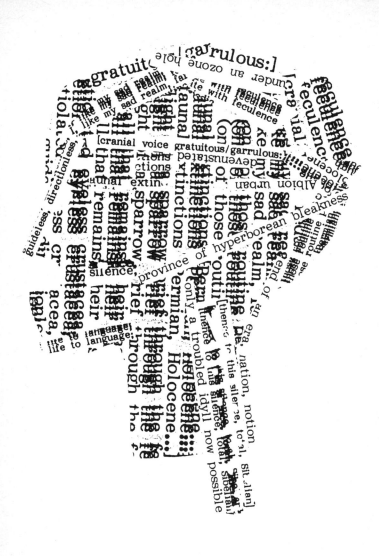

[cranial voice gratuitous/garrulous:]

region of hyperborean bleakness;

cranial voice loquacious/inadequate

feebly { translating life to language;

reducing

I, like my sad realm, farctate with feculence

(one of those routine periodic

faunal extinctions [Permian, Holocene...],

flight of a sparrow brief through the feasting hall);

all that remains, their last year's shit's stench;

etiolated eyeless crustacea,

guideless, directionless, lightless, silent

[thence to this silence, total, Siberian]

Midwinter feast, crammed stalls in a market-place;
        vendors of steaming gewürzy glühwein;
over a pine blaze, sputtering griddled wursts;
easterly sleet blast lashing the flanks of freak
beasts in a side-show – muzzled, incongruous
        Indian elephant, dromedary;

ratskeller clamour, warm odoriferous
    waftings from baked eel, roast goose, wildschwein
    basted with pears in portugieser;

babel of strange-tongued wanderers; slumping in
    schweinschmalz, a Northman, soused in weisswein,
        incomprehensibly stutters slurred dirge:

        Quondam Parnassian, muse prolific,
    Master of Troubled Idyll, charted
        province of hyperborean bleakness. . .
fell into silence, like great Sibelius
mute till the end, reflective of soundlessness.

All that remains, the stench of their excrement.

sea-level newly pole-augmented,
mutated arthropods, algae, UV,
force 12s dispersing disbound **Collected Works**

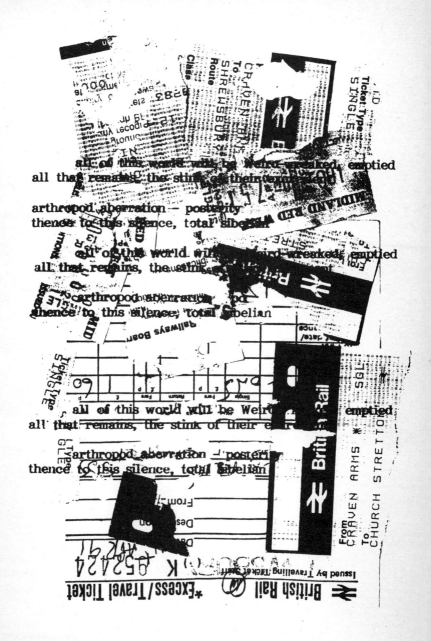

...e and is likely ... ...
craft to find the heliopause.
Voyager will be hurtling through
space searching for the
heliopause — the interface where
the Sun's influence ends and in-
terstellar space begins.

... explorers to cross this fence
— by the year 2010 or 2020, when
they may still have almost 10 years
of contact with the Earth before
they run out of power.
Voyager 1 aft...

... This boundary marks the edge
of the solar winds, where the energy and atomic particles stream-
ing out from the Sun cease, and
has never been ... ...
Earth ... ...

...eyond the year 2020, the plu-
...nium-based generators on
board the spacecraft will give too
little power to keep the Voyagers
operating as explorers, but they
will continue to hurtle through
the Milky Way. In 40,000 years
time, Voyager 1 will meet the star
AC+79 3888, in the northern
constellation of Camelopardalis.

... ... time, Voyager
will encounter Ross 248, and
some 250,000 years later the star
Sirius. But these "encounters"
will be at distances of trillions of
miles from the stars, rather than
... ... Voyager ...

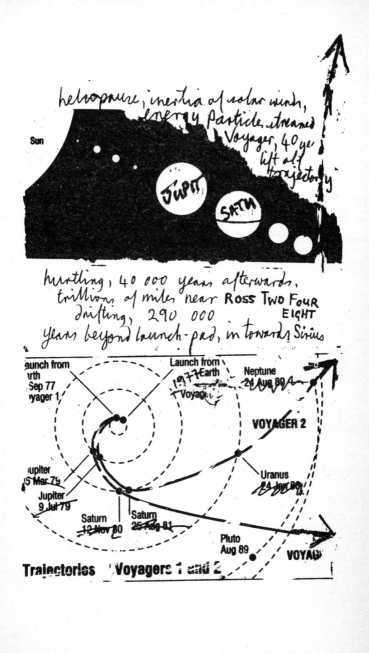

heliopause, inertia of solar winds,
energy Particle streamed
Voyager, 40 years
lift off
trajectory

Sun

JUPIT SATU

hurtling, 40 000 years afterwards,
trillions of miles near ROSS TWO FOUR
drifting, 290 000   EIGHT
years beyond launch-pad, in towards Sirius

aunch from
rth
Sep 77
yager 1

Launch from
Earth
1977
Voyag

Neptune
24 Aug 89

VOYAGER 2

Jupiter
5 Mar 79

Jupiter
9 Jul 79

Saturn
12 Nov 80

Saturn
25 Aug 81

Uranus
24 Jan 86

Pluto
Aug 89

VOYAG

Trajectories Voyagers 1 and 2

heliopause, inertia of solar winds,
        energy particles streamed from Sun cease,
    Voyager, 40 years since lift-off,
        power from plutonium generator
greatly reduced, continues trajectory,

hurtling, 40 000 years afterwards,
    trillions of miles near Ross 248,

        drifting, 290 000
years beyond launch-pad, in towards Sirius